Township of Smith-Ennismore-Lakefield
Fire Department
P.O. Box 270 Bridgenorth, Ontario K0L 1H0
Phone 705-292-7282 Fax 705-292-8634

The Township of South-Ennismore-Lakefield Fire Department was founded in January 2001. It consists of three Municipalities that were combined due to Provincial Legislation. The Townships of Smith and Ennismore were originally amalgamated on January 1, 1998. With Lakefield becoming part of the final Municipality on January 1,2001.

The department now consists of five fire halls, Hall #1 in Bridgenorth, Hall #2 in the Village of Lakefield, Hall #3 in Youngs Point, Hall #4 on Curve Lake Road and Hall #5 in Ennismore. Together they cover an area of 158 sq. miles (409 sq. km) including water as the Township is surrounded by a number of Lakes and a river that is in the Kawartha Lakes and Trent Severn Waterway systems. The fire halls house a number of pieces of apparatus including; 9 pumper tankers, 1-3,000 gallon super tanker, 4 rescue response units, 3 fire boats (1 -14' zodiak. 1-18' air boat, 1-18' flat bottom).

This apparatus includes equipment for a vast array of emergency responses (ice, water rescue, motor vehicle extrication, medical assists, carbon monoxide alarms) to name a few.

The department consists of 90 volunteer firefighters. Members are assigned to the five halls for response to these areas that need emergency assistance.

These volunteers give their time to answer those emergency calls at all and any time of the day, in all weather. Many times we take for granted the time and effort that is invested for calls and the training needed to do the job. Firefighters' spouses are the backbone of their department, as it is these individuals who tirelessly look after all that is important in our lives to allow the firefighters to respond to help the community. There are also a number of businesses in the community that allow their employees to attend to emergency calls during business hours, for this unselfish effort we thank you.

A major function of the department, which this book is a part of is the Fire Safety education and ongoing Fire Prevention inspections in the community that help keep our residences, fire safe. From pre-schoolers to our seniors, fire safety cannot be stressed enough. The goals of education programs are to help minimize injuries and loss of life, due to the result of fires. I am pleased to take this opportunity to thank the many sponsors of this fire safety book. Your contributions will help in our long-term goals in producing a fire safe community for our residences.

Yours in Service

Gord Jopling
Fire Chief

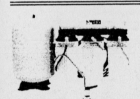

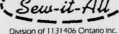

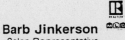

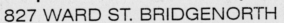

NOTICE TO THE READER

The aim of this book is to bring to children a fundamental knowledge of many of the fire safety issues that they could encounter in their young lives. The book is written in clear, simple terms that are easy for children to read and understand. As well, the topics are divided into sections for quick reference. Content for the book was gathered from numerous sources including interviews with fire fighters.

The editor, author, consultants and publisher of this book do not accept responsibility for the consequences from the use of any treatment, action, or the application of any suggestion made in this book.

ISBN #   1-55056-892-2
Children's Programs
Jewett, TX / Wpg., MB
1-800-447-8374
Web Site: www.childrensprograms.net

Author: Virginia Sperl
Editor: Charlene Natyna, Carla McIntyre
Contributors:Fire Fighters Historical Society of Winnipeg (Barb & Ted Kuryluk, George Treddenick)
Interior Illustrations: Fraser C. Koch
Cover Artwork: Accu-Graphics
Printed and bound in Canada by Friesens

Other books published by the Children's Programs are "Sick But Not Scared," a children's health book to help alleviate the fears of the unknown; "Tiny Step Stories," a book of short stories with a moral written by authors from around the country; "Heart of a Champion" which contains inspirational stories of people who have overcome adversity and "Look Listen Learn" a children's all around safety book.

To all fire fighters:
If you have a real life story or other items that you think would fit in this book please call us as we are constantly adding material to the numerous revisions.

Index

Stories with Fire Safety Messages

Ole Owl Fire Tips(Must Read)

So You Want to be a Firefighter

True Firefighter Stories

HOT COALS

Shivering uncontrollably, Brian hops up and down by the front door attempting to remove his soaking wet socks. Once his cold toes are free, the ten-year-old rushes into the living room and cuddles up to the fireplace, feet first and releases a deep sigh of relief.

Playing hockey outside with his friends is a lot of fun but somehow Brian always manages to get his socks wet. Maybe because when he sits down on the park bench to take his skates off, he somehow forgets where he is for a moment and steps into the soft white snow before putting his feet in his winter boots, causing the snow to melt and his socks to get wet.

"Here's your hot chocolate, honey." Said his mother as she placed the warm mug and a plate of cookies on the coffee table, and gently kissed his forehead." "Now remember, don't get too close to the fireplace Brian because sometimes the

sparks can fly out and they might burn you."

Brian nodded in agreement, not really paying too much attention to her words. A warning he had heard many times before.

After his mother had returned to the kitchen, Brian finished off the last sip of hot chocolate. He then licked his finger and dragged it along the plate to make sure all the cookie crumbs would stick, before putting it into his mouth. Rubbing his full tummy, Brian looked down to his feet and wiggled all his toes to make sure all ten were nice and warm.

Glancing over at the fire, the small boy noticed that it had burned down to just glowing coals. He decided to get the poker that sat beside the fireplace and move around the logs to help the flames grow higher. Brian had seen his father do this many times before but unfortunately his mind seemed to have forgotten his parent's rule about not touching the fireplace; only sit and enjoy it.

While aimlessly poking and prodding the bright red coals and grey ashes, the warmth of the fire on his face was making him feel a little drowsy.

As Brian moved his poker around the logs, not really paying careful attention to what he was doing, he failed to notice an ember that jumped out of the fireplace and onto the carpet beside him. It didn't take long before he could feel the heat underneath his leg and when he looked down, he saw a little puff of smoke billowing up. "Mom, I'm on *fire!*" screamed the frightened boy as he attempted to stand up. As soon as the air reached the carpet, a bright red flame shot up with more to follow.

His mother came running in from the kitchen and when she saw the situation, she immediately told her son to "STOP! DROP! AND ROLL!

4

Brian quickly remembered this lesson from school and did as she said. As her son began to roll back and forth on the floor, she grabbed the closest flower vase, swiftly throwing the water onto the carpet in an effort to extinguish the flames. Once she realized the situation was under control, she immediately drew her attention to her son and saw that he had successfully smothered his pant leg. When Brian looked up at his mother, he began to cry for two reasons. One because he was frightened by what had just happened, and two because he knew the fire had been his fault.

His mother reached down and scooped up her weeping child in her arms, gently rocking him back and forth, until he calmed down. "Brian, we were lucky this time but this could have been a lot worse. You know the rules about playing with the fireplace," she whispered. Brian slowly nodded his head and the both of them knew he would never play with the coals again. His parents also made another rule in the house. Brian was not to be left unattended when the fireplace was on, and that was one rule Brian was happy to live by.

The End

SMOKING CABIN

The Christmas party was in full gear! The guests were gathered in small groups throughout the main floor of the house. Some were busy filling their plates with goodies in the dining room, some were seated in the living room laughing at all the stories being shared, and some folks were in the den playing cards and smoking cigarettes. This was the only room in the house where Melissa's parents allowed smoking.

Melissa, being the big sister at six-years-old was in charge of entertaining her three-year-old little brother, Jamie. They were excited about being able to watch their favorite movie video in their parent's bedroom and eat potato chips. Their mom had made a deal with her daughter before the guests arrived, that once Jamie had fallen fast asleep upstairs, Melissa could come downstairs to the party for a few minutes and say hello to everyone.

Soon Jamie's eyes were shut tight and his teddy bear was held snuggly in his arms as he slept peacefully in his parent's bed. Melissa then pulled her robe tightly around her and tip-toed downstairs to the kitchen. Standing outside the door, the little girl watched how busy her mother was preparing the food for her guests. "Poor mom, she looks like she could use some help," thought Melissa as she began to weave in and out of people and clear away the dirty plates and glasses. Returning to the kitchen, she put the paper plates and napkins in the garbage can and the glasses in the sink.

"Thank you darling, you have been a big help but now I think it's time you went on up to bed," said her mother as she hugged her daughter and returned to her guests in the living room. While on her way upstairs, Melissa past by the den and noticed all the ashtrays were almost overflowing with cigarette butts. "I'll just do one more thing to help mommy before I go to bed," smiled the young girl as she gathered up the full ashtrays and snuck into the kitchen. She quickly dumped the grey ashes and cigarettes butts into the garbage can right on top of the paper plates and napkins she had thrown away earlier that

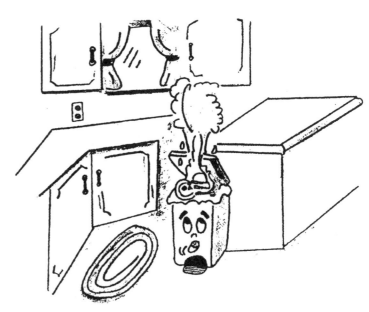

evening. "Yuck! That stinks!" she said as she curled up her nose and closed the lid of the garbage can. Trotting off to bed, Melissa was feeling very proud of herself for helping out.

Long after the guests had left and her parents had wearily tucked themselves into bed, the house suddenly began to scream with the high-pitched sound of the smoke detector going off. Melissa's eyes popped opened and it only took her a few moments to realize what that noise meant.

Remembering her families many fire drills, the young girl quickly tried to calm her crying little brother, while she carefully went to the bedroom door and touched the handle to see if it was hot. Greatly relieved to find the door knob cool to the touch, she slowly opened the door and peered down the hall. Just then she saw her mother running down the hall

7

towards them in her housecoat and slippers. "It's okay kids. Everything is under control. Daddy took care of it," she said as she hugged both children tightly, trying not to show them how shaken she was.

The three of them walked downstairs and Melissa could see a faint cloud of smoke hanging in the air. As her father quickly moved around the living room and kitchen opening windows for fresh air, Melissa asked what happened. "I think a guest may have dumped an ashtray full of cigarettes into the garbage can that was full of paper plates and napkins. One of the cigarettes must not have been completely extinguished and a spark from the end of it ignited a napkin or plate, starting a fire.

Immediately Melissa's stomach began not to feel well and she could feel a large lump forming in her throat. Her eyes swelled with tears and she began crying loudly. "It's my fault! I'm the one that put the ashtray in the garbage can. I thought I was helping mommy. I didn't mean to start a fire!" sobbed the little girl as she buried her head in her mother's housecoat.

When Melissa's little brother saw his sister so upset, he also began crying. Their father bent down and picked up Jamie, cradling him in his arms. "Calm down you two, we were lucky this time but do you see how fast fires can start? This one could have been a lot worse but the smoke detectors warned us in time, and we were able to avoid a dangerous situation. Next time you would like to help us out Melissa, please ask first, okay?' smiled her father. Melissa felt better and nodded her head in agreement and they all returned to bed and finished off their night's sleep.

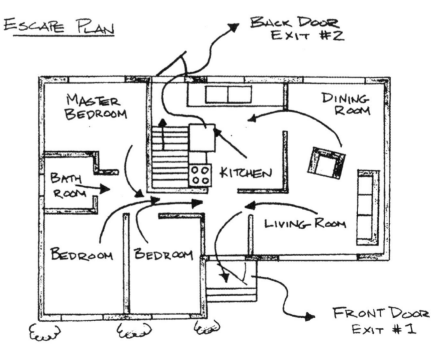

THE END

8

HAPPY BIRTHDAY!

The dining room table looked lovely. Mom had spent most of the afternoon decorating it with her favorite linen table cloth, matching napkins and antique silver candle holders. The twins, Jeremy & Jennie were very excited about celebrating their ninth birthday. Their mother had fixed their favorite meal-fried chicken, mashed potatoes with gravy and fresh buns. But the best part was going to be the double, chocolate cake with candy sprinkles for dessert!

Laughter could be heard throughout the house as the family gathered around the table and shared many jokes and stories. "Okay, time to clear the table for dessert," said mother as she, their father and older brother John stood up and began taking dirty dishes into the kitchen. "Now you two be good and we'll be back in a jiffy with dessert," their father said as he disappeared into the kitchen.

Jeremy looked across the table at Jenny with a little devilish smile. "I bet you one dollar that I can put my finger through the candle flame," he wagered. "Are you crazy? Mom & Dad will be so mad at you for playing with the candles. Do you know how much trouble you're going to be in if you get caught?" asked Jenny. Staring at the flickering flame of the candle, Jeremy replied. "Not if I do it quickly before anyone comes back."

Jeremy stuck out his pointer finger and quickly brushed it through the golden flame. Proudly displaying his finger that was now blackened from the soot of the fire, Jenny's brother now challenged her to do the same. "See how easy that was, and I didn't feel a thing. Your turn!" Peeking down the hall, Jenny could hear the rest of the family busily preparing the plates and forks for dessert. "Okay! Okay! I'll do it but we have to hurry because they'll be back in one minute," said Jenny, nervously reaching out to the candle in front of her. As her finger began to slide through the flame, Jenny heard footsteps coming towards the dining room.

Panicking, she jerked her finger back, accidentally knocking over the candle onto the linen table cloth. Immediately the flames began shooting up from the table just as her parents entered the room. Her mother and father instantly grabbed the water and milk glasses and threw them onto the fire, extinguishing the flames and a puff of grey smoke rose up from the burnt table cloth.

"Look at my Grandmother's tablecloth! This is an antique! What have you two done?" cried their mother as she gathered up the scorched linen. Jenny and Jeremy felt awful for making their mother cry and they too began to sob. "We're sorry mom; we didn't mean to wreck it," said Jeremy.

"How many times have we told you two not to play with fire?" scolded their father. "You're lucky we came in here when we did. This fire could have done a lot more damage and you could have been badly burnt! Fire has to be respected and only used safely."He said as they all finished cleaning up the mess.

"We're really sorry." The twins replied. "We knew we weren't supposed to fool around with the candles and we promise it won't happen again," said Jenny. The family then sat back down at the table and watched quietly as mother began preparing the plates and forks for the cake. As she looked at the candles on the birthday cake, she picked up the matches and looked at the twins with a smile on her face.

"So, do you think we can light the candles on the cake without you two trying to burn down the house?" she giggled. "We have definitely learned our lesson for today," said Jeremy "No more playing with fire, we promise!" he said as he glanced over to Jenny who was nodding her head in agreement.

"Let's continue with your party and be thankful only the table cloth was ruined," said their father as everyone cheerfully began eating chocolate cake.

HAPPY MOTHER'S DAY!

Jim and Sandy decided to wake up early in the morning and make their mom chocolate chip pancakes for a surprise Mother's Day breakfast.

Jim was twelve-years-old and quite responsible for his age. Their father didn't live with the family, so the young boy took it upon himself to be the man around the house and help out his mother whenever he could.

His ten-year-old younger sister, Sandy also took turns with the chores but cooking was always her favorite thing to do.

This particular morning the children set their alarm and were full of excitement in anticipation of cooking breakfast by themselves. It was Sandy's idea for the chocolate chip pancakes and Jim's idea for the extra crispy bacon that would accompany them.

As Sandy quietly read the instructions on the box of pancakes and measured the ingredients before pouring them into the mixing bowls, she and her mother had made pancakes many times before, so Sandy felt confident about cooking them by herself this time. As Jim lifted the big cast iron frying pan onto the stove, Sandy looked over at him and said "Mom always makes the bacon in the microwave and not in a frying pan." "I know but I think it tastes better on the stove than in the microwave," he replied.

"Okay but be careful because you've never cooked bacon before," said Sandy, returning her attention to stirring the batter in the bowl.

Turning on the element, Jim neatly placed six strips of bacon in the pan and waited for them to begin cooking. Ten minutes later, Sandy scooped up the last fluffy pancake oozing with chocolate chips and placed it onto the plate. Turning the element off, she carefully put the hot pan in a sink of cold water, allowing it to soak. "Okay, I'm ready, where's the bacon?" Sandy asked Jim before heading upstairs.

"I'm coming" he replied as he quickly took the prongs from the utensil drawer and plucked crispy strips of bacon from their greasy pool in the frying pan and plopped them onto an awaiting paper towel. After positioning the bacon in straight lines on the plate, Jim rushed up the stairs to join his sister in surprising their mother with breakfast.

"Happy Mother's Day!" the children shouted as they proudly entered her bedroom with plates of food in their hands. Propping herself up in bed, a large smile spread across their mother's face and her eyes began to swell with tears. "You two cooked me breakfast? This is such a wonderful treat," she said as Jim and Sandy leaned forward to receive a hug.

But before their mother could even finish her first bite of the pancake, they were all jolted by the shrilling sound of the smoke detector going off downstairs. Jim instantly noticed the strong stench of something burning. As their mother hopped out of bed and wrapped her robe around her, she turned to her children and asked "Did you two remember to turn everything off in the kitchen?"

As Sandy answered yes with certainty, Jim found himself trying desperately to remember if he also turned the element off under the frying pan. "I, I don't know if I did." Jim answered as he began to feel his knees quiver.

Leading her children carefully down the smoke filled staircase, their mother then directed them to go to the neighbors and phone 911 for help. "I'll be right there, I just want to see how bad the situation is first," she said as she headed for the kitchen.

Jim had indeed forgotten to turn the stove off and the bacon grease had ignited. The flames had found the greasy paper towels that had been placed on the countertop next to the stove. Realizing she had to act quickly before the fire spread even further, mom grabbed the silver tongs that were resting beside the plate, picked up the paper towels and carefully tossed them directly into the sink of cold water that Sandy had her pan soaking in. Clutching the lid to the frying pan, she

immediately placed it on top and smothered the flames, ensuring to shut off the burner and allow the pan to completely cool before removing it.

Unfortunately, before one of the flames was extinguished, it had a chance to burn her hand, As she was running cold water from the tap over her injured hand, firemen came rushing through the opened front door, stopping at the entrance of the kitchen. "Looks like you have everything under control." Said the Fire Captain as his eyes scanned the room to make sure there were no other potential fire hazards.

Most of the smoke had disappeared and only the mess remained. One of the firemen came over and began to attend to their mother's wounds as Jim and Sandy slowly walked into the house. Jim was very upset and felt quite guilty for what he had done. The Fire Captain sat both of the kids down at the kitchen table and explained how this fire could have been avoided.

Once all the excitement had settled down and everyone had left, their mother turned and said "I think we all learned a valuable lesson today about how fast and easily fires can start. I do appreciate what you both tried to do for me today, but how about from now on let me do the cooking?" Jim & Sandy smiled in agreement and gave her a big hug. "I've got a great idea!" piped up mom. "Let's get dressed and order a pizza! I think we have missed breakfast and lunch today and I'm starving!"

HOT MITTS!

Eight-year-old Natalie loved playing in the snow. As soon as she spied the first white snowflake gently float down from the grey sky above and land on her front lawn, she would have her winter coat, snow pants, boots and mitts fastened tightly around her and out the front door she flew.

One lazy afternoon in the middle of winter, Natalie was beginning to feel tired and hungry after making her eleventh snow angel in her yard. She decided to go inside and warm up with a snack.

After hanging up her coat and pants, she put her snow covered boots on the rubber mat. Feeling very tired, she decided to put her soaking wet mitts and hat on the heat register that sat beside the hall closet. She knew very well that her mother and father had told her not to ever do that because they may catch on fire from the heat of the register.

But today she thought it would only be a few moments while she drank her cider and went back outside to play. Peeking down the hall to make sure her parents didn't see her, she tip-toed into the kitchen and reached into the cookie jar. Placing four cookies on a plate and grabbing a glass of chocolate milk, she trotted off to watch a movie and enjoy her snack.

Just as she had settled into her favorite big cozy chair, her mother entered the room. "Hi honey, we didn't hear you come in. Did you put away all your wet clothes?" she asked. Nodding her head, Natalie answered. "Yes, but I'm going back outside as soon as I finish my cookies." "Okay, but don't eat too many because dinner will be in an hour or so," her mother said as she left the room.

14

Finishing her last bite of cookie, Natalie could feel her eyes becoming very heavy, and before she knew it, she had dozed off to sleep. An hour later her mother awoke her for dinner. "I think after dinner you should go to bed and catch up on your sleep," she said to her daughter as she rubbed her sleepy eyes. Natalie had completely forgotten about her mitts and hat that she had placed on the heat register hours earlier and her mother didn't think to check to see if her daughter had in fact put everything away.

Several hours later as the family peacefully slept, the mitts and hat that were sitting on the heat register began to smolder and catch on fire. The house slowly began to fill with smoke. Her mother and father were startled awake with the smell and immediately crawled out of bed and across the bedroom floor. Stretching out his arm to touch the door knob, Natalie's father was greatly relieved to find it was cool. Now knowing the fire was not right outside their bedroom door, he slowly opened it and peered down the hall. Noticing that it was completely filled with smoke, he knew he had to act fast and reach Natalie's room.

Her mother began shouting for her daughter to wake up as her father rushed into her room and scooped her up into his arms. A very groggy Natalie began to cough as she inhaled some of the smoke lingering in the hallway. Rushing towards the front door, her father immediately realized the fire had started by the register and they quickly turned and exited out the back door to safety.

Cold and frightened, the family huddled together in the front yard and watched as the firefighters rushed into their home and quickly extinguished the fire. Natalie knew instantly how the fire must have started and she began to cry when she explained it to her parents. Although they were angry, her parents were more relieved that everyone got out safe and sound. The Fire Captain approached the three of them and gently discussed their findings. Looking down at the young girl, he said "I hope you understand how careful we have to be around registers and how fast fires can start. It's a good thing your smoke detectors were working and gave you an early warning. Inhaling smoke can be just as dangerous as the flames."

Natalie had learned a valuable lesson that day, as did her parents. Before bed, everything was checked to make sure things like the stove was turned off and nothing flammable was placed near the register.

THE END

FULL POWER!

Johnny was so excited about opening the biggest birthday present from his uncle at his party. He was hoping for the race car he had picked out months earlier. As he quickly ripped off the brightly colored wrapping paper, he squealed in delight when he saw the shiny red hood of the car.

"I love it! I love it! It's exactly what I wanted Uncle Dan! Thank you! Thank you!" said Johnny as he climbed out of his chair with his new car and placed it on the floor. Standing above, he turned the remote control left and right making his red car turn in all directions. "Well, I guess the party is over," his mom laughed as she and Uncle Dan began clearing off the dishes from the table. Johnny spent most of the afternoon driving the car all over the house. Under the kitchen table, over the couch pillows and through the dog's legs went the red car until it began to drive slower and slower.

"What's wrong with it Uncle Dan?" asked Johnny. Uncle Dan carefully looked at the car and said "I think the batteries have died. We'll have to go to the store tomorrow and buy some new ones."
"Tomorrow! I can't wait until then! I want to drive it now!" cried Johnny. "Sorry Johnny but the stores are closed for the night." Said Uncle Dan as he turned and left the room.

Once Johnny had finished crying he began thinking about where he could get his hands on some more batteries. Looking up, he said "I know. The smoke detector has the same kind of batteries as my car. I'll just take them out of there for tonight and put them back in tomorrow after I go to the store and buy new ones."

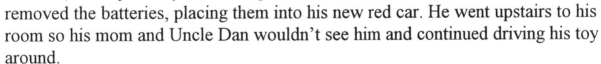
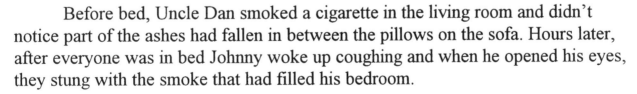

Pulling the chair under the smoke detector, Johnny slowly climbed up and removed the batteries, placing them into his new red car. He went upstairs to his room so his mom and Uncle Dan wouldn't see him and continued driving his toy around.

Before bed, Uncle Dan smoked a cigarette in the living room and didn't notice part of the ashes had fallen in between the pillows on the sofa. Hours later, after everyone was in bed Johnny woke up coughing and when he opened his eyes, they stung with the smoke that had filled his bedroom.

Alarmed and frightened, he remembered the rules of fire safety his mom had taught him. Crawling over to the door, he touched the knob and noticed it was cool. Covering his mouth with his pajama sleeve, he opened his door and ran down the hall to his mother's room. Passing the living room he realized the sofa was on fire. "Mom, get up! There's a fire in the living room!"

17

His mother jumped out of bed. "Johnny, run outside to the meeting tree and I'll be right there! She said. Johnny did as he was told and waited for his mom to come out. When she saw the fire in the living room, his mother grabbed the phone and called 911 before running outside to join her son.

After the firemen had put out the fire, they checked the smoke alarm and informed Johnny's mom that there was no battery in it. "That's impossible. I always make sure the battery is working." She said in a startled voice. Johnny looked up at her and said "I took the battery out of it today so I could run my race car. I'm really sorry mom."

Johnny learned a very important lesson that day. Never remove batteries from smoke detectors!

PARK PAPER

Ten-year-old Nathan and his twelve-year-old sister Kelly were bored. It was noon on Saturday and they had already played every video game, two board games, and cards and watched all their favorite Saturday morning cartoons.

"Why don't you two go to the park? It's a beautiful day outside," suggested their mother, as she began preparing dinner in the kitchen.

Nathan shrugged his shoulders in continued boredom but Kelly's eyes lit up and she gave her brother a devilish grin. "That's a great idea Mom! See you later. We'll be back in time for dinner." She said as she grabbed her brother's shirt sleeve and dragged him out the back door.

Once outside Nathan turned to his sister and said "Since when do you like hanging out with me at the park? I thought you were too cool to go to the park now?" he giggled as they strolled through the park pathway that led to the duck pond.

Kelly reached into her pocket and pulled out a bright red lighter. "I feel like having some fun. Come on!" she yelled as she bolted away from her brother towards the picnic tables. Scanning the area, Kelly was pleased no one was around. Nathan finally caught up, huffing and puffing. "What are you doing with Dad's lighter? You know we're not allowed to play with it." Nathan instructed.

"Nathan, you're such a rule person. Sometimes it's fun to break the rules now and then. Especially if you don't get caught," she said as she spied a garbage can full of trash. Pointing the lighter directly at a piece of plastic sitting on the top of the pile, she tried flicking the lighter with her thumb, attempting to get a flame.

Nathan nervously checked over both of his shoulders to ensure no one was coming. "Finally!" smiled Kelly as a small flame popped out of the end of the lighter and made contact with the plastic. Instantly the plastic began to shrivel and melt and the flame disappeared. Nathan let out a large sigh of relief when he saw the fire had gone out. "Okay, you had your fun Kelly, now put the lighter away and let's go to the swing sets," he said as he started walking away.

"Wait little brother, the fun has just begun," Kelly piped up as she pointed to the garbage can that now had flames climbing higher and higher out of it.

"How did that happen?" asked Nathan. "The heat and flame from the plastic must have caught the other garbage underneath it on fire. Cool huh?" asked Kelly feeling very proud of her accomplishment.

Before Nathan could answer, his eyes widened with fear when he saw the flames building higher and higher. The garbage can was now a raging fire and the two kids knew they had lost control of the situation.

Kelly began to freak out and tried putting the fire out by blowing on it which only made it worst because more oxygen fueled the flames. "Do something Kelly!" yelled Nathan.

Two adults passing by noticed the trouble the kids were in and immediately rushed to their aid. "Get away from the fire! !" called out the lady as her husband

ran over to another garbage can and quickly tipped it upside down to empty it. He then jumped over the small fence that surrounded the duck pond and placed the can in the water. Once it was filled, he rushed over to the flaming can and carefully poured the water on it, snuffing out the fire.

As Kelly and Nathan stood trembling, the man turned to them and asked for the lighter or matches that started the fire. "You realize how bad this could have been if we hadn't arrived when we did, don't you?" the man angrily asked the children. "1 hope you learned a lesson here because the next time you may not be so lucky with someone showing up to help you out. The next time you may get badly hurt trying to put a fire out by yourself."

Before Kelly could answer, he and his wife turned away in disgust, leaving her feeling embarrassed and ashamed. In barely a whisper, she thanked them for their help. Putting her arm around Nathan, the two quietly walked home thinking about how easily fires can start and how frightening they can be.

The End

HAIR TODAY, GONE TOMORROW

Daniel wasn't a very popular grade six student. Things weren't great at home with his family and he always seemed to feel angry about something. He always managed to get into trouble at school but no matter what he did, he never intentionally tried to hurt anybody.

The only thing that really seemed to hold Daniel's interest was fire. He was fascinated by the color of the blue and orange flames and how easily he had the

power to start small fires.

Most of the fires he started were harmless, he felt. He would sit in the field behind his house and light dry grass. He always managed to put the fire out before it got too large.

One particular November afternoon at school, Daniel was feeling more than usually irritated. The kids had been teasing him all morning about his greasy hair and dirty clothes. Justine Clarkson had made cruel remarks about him all science class. Justine was the most popular girl in grade six with her long blonde hair and emerald green eyes. Whenever she said something, a group of followers would always agree and laugh along.

Unfortunately, Justine picked the wrong day to bug Daniel. He had had enough of her mean comments, and after lunch as she was getting her books out of her locker, Daniel quietly walked by and with a quick flick of his lighter, a flame jumped out and attached itself to the bottom of the young girl's long hair.

Instantly the smell of burnt hair filled the hallway and a group of kids that had witnessed Daniel's deed, ran towards him and held him for the arrival of the principal. Justine began screaming with fright as her friend smacked her math book on her back to put the fire out on her hair.

Daniel immediately felt bad. He didn't mean to hurt her, but only to scare her with the sound of the lighter flicking. He didn't think the lighter was close enough to do any damage.

Seated in the principal's office waiting for his parents to arrive, Daniel knew he was in big trouble.

His head lowered in shame, he said "I'm sorry. I really didn't mean to hurt her." Although Daniel was suspended from school for a few days, and had to receive counseling for his anger, the thrill of fire no longer excited him. He learned it wasn't funny to hurt people.

The End

FIELD OF DREAMS

Pressing his hands tightly against his ears, nine-year-old Jordan was still unable to tune-out his parent's arguing. A small tear began to trickle down his cheek, and at that instant, Jordan decided to get away from the constant bickering in his house.

Quietly sliding up his bedroom window, Jordan managed to pop out his screen and jump outside. He ran like the wind across the open field until his legs could no longer carry him. Collapsing in exhaustion, he lay on a grassy blanket staring up into the sunny blue sky. Focusing on a puffy white cloud, Jordan imagined himself as a bird being able to fly far away from his parents and their fighting.

"Jordan is that you?" shouted his friend Kyle as he quickly rode up on his bike. "What are you doing out here in the middle of the field?" he asked as he hopped off of his bike and watched it fall to the ground. Although Kyle knew the answer before Jordan even replied. All the neighbors in this close farm community knew of Jordan's parents fighting.

"Hey, I know how to cheer you up! Follow me and let's have some fun!" said Kyle as he pulled Jordan up from the ground and the two boys doubled on his bike to a nearby ditch.

Walking over to a bush, Kyle dug around for a few moments before pulling out an old rusted red gas can. "Where did you get that?" asked Jordan.

"My Dad has tons of these cans around the farm. He won't even notice one missing," Kyle replied as he began to slowly pour the gasoline in a straight line down the grassy filled ditch. "How are you going to put it out ?" asked Jordan. Kyle pointed to a small body of water pooling in the ditch about two feet away. "When we're ready, we'll just scoop some water out with the empty can and put out the fire. Simple, huh?" Kyle asked his friend. Jordan felt unsure of the situation, but decided to go along.

After Kyle poured the gasoline along the ditch, he and Jordan stood back while Kyle threw a lit match on the soaked grass. The ditch immediately made a 'HUFF' sound and the flames were roaring.

The two boys looked in awe as the flames took on a life of their own, but before they knew it, the fire was spreading out of control. Kyle reached down and picked up the empty can of gasoline and started filling it up with water.

But what he didn't realize was that the can still had a little bit of gasoline inside, so when Kyle threw it onto the fire, it only made it grow larger. Baffled by what was happening, the boys jumped back and Kyle dropped the can into the water they were now standing in.

In a blink of an eye, the fire was traveling right towards them. Kyle quickly jumped out of the ditch to the side of the road but Jordan's reaction was not quite as fast. He felt a hot sensation and looked down to see his runner was smoking.

"My runner is on fire!" he screamed as he hopped up to the road, frantically trying to kick his smoldering runner off. Kyle reached down and scooped up a large handful of sand and gravel, throwing it onto the runner, trying to put the fire out. They then both took off down the road to call for help.

The local volunteer fire department rushed to the scene and was successful in putting the fire out. The ditch was black and smoke filled the nearby woods. The two boys sat on the grass nearby, feeling terrible for what they had done. After the Fire Chief reprimanded them for being so careless, they were told they had to do twelve hours of community work. The boys had to go to the fire hall and wash the trucks, mop the floors and see how important it is not to waste the fireman's time with senseless fires.

THE END

KEEP GAS AWAY FROM THE FURNACE!

LAMP SHADE

Tina was such a slob! She couldn't even tell you the color of her carpet because she couldn't see it with the amount of dirty clothes she had strewn all over. Each day her mother would fumble her way in the dark to wake up Tina for school and each day her mother would say "Tina, I want you to clean your room right after school. It looks like a disaster in here!" And each day Tina would nod in agreement, still rubbing the sleep from her eyes.

One day, while Tina was busy painting her nails a bright blue color, something

caught her attention out of the corner of her eye. Smoke was coming from her lamp! At least she thought it was her lamp but she wasn't sure because there was a towel from the bathroom thrown over it. She immediately began to panic and ran downstairs to tell her mom.

Her mother ran into her room, stumbling over her numerous piles of clothing and quickly grabbed the end of the towel and tossed it onto the floor. The weight of the bath towel had pushed the lampshade onto the lit light bulb and the heat caused the plastic lampshade to melt.

27

"Okay young lady. This should be a lesson to you to clean your room. If you had left the lamp on and gone out, we could have had a fire and the house could have burned down," her mother lectured as she wagged her finger in Tina's face. Tina surveyed her room and agreed that from now on she would put away her clothes and prevent anything more from becoming a potential fire hazard in her room.

The End

Ole Owl Says This Section Must Be Read

Home Safe Home

Is your home fire safe?

Ask a grown-up to help you complete this checklist.

◊ Does your home have at least one smoke alarm on every floor?
◊ Have you replaced the batteries in your smoke alarm this year?
◊ If you have a fireplace, does it have doors or a screen?
◊ Do your electrical outlets have no more than two cords plugged into them?
◊ Are all electrical cords in good shape? (Damaged cords are a fire hazard.)
◊ Are matches and lighters kept in a safe place?
◊ If you have a space heater, is it kept away from walls, drapes, furniture and bedding?
◊ Are pot handles on the stove always turned in so they don't get knocked over?
◊ Is the iron always unplugged and put away in a safe place when it's not being used?
◊ Is there always a grown-up in the room when candles are burning?

Where Do Your Smoke Alarms Go?

 Here are some suggestions that will help you install your smoke alarms in the locations which will best protect you and your family. Minimum safety requirements suggest that smoke alarms be installed outside every sleeping area and on every level of the home, including the basement. For extra protection, the Office of the Fire Marshall recommends that one be installed in the dining room, living room, utility room and in hallways. If your family sleeps with the bedroom door closed, it is important to install a smoke alarm inside the bedroom. Smoke alarms installed in the basement should be at the bottom of the stairway which leads to the floor above. Smoke alarms should be mounted on the ceiling approximately 15 centimeters (six inches) from the wall. Do not put smoke alarms at the top of stairways - dead air spaces may hamper smoke from reaching the smoke alarm and result in a delayed warning in case of fire.

Maintaining Your Smoke Alarm.

Test your smoke alarms every month by pressing and holding the test button for a few seconds. The alarm should sound immediately. If a smoke alarm does not have a test button, it is probably an older, obsolete model and should be replaced. You should replace your smoke alarms at leave every 10 years. Replace your smoke alarm's battery at least once a year, more often if necessary.

A good reminder is: Change your clock - Change your battery!

Don't be a battery bandit - never remove the battery from a smoke alarm for any other use! If your smoke alarm is beeping sporadically, it could be in need of cleaning.

How to Develop a Fire Escape Plan.

1. Install smoke alarms on each floor of your home and test them regularly.
2. Draw a floor plan of your home showing all possible exits from each room.
3. Where possible, plan a main exit route and an alternate exit route from each room.
4. Make certain that everyone understands that if they hear the smoke alarm, or hear someone shouting "fire" they should immediately evacuate the home.
5. Decide on a meeting place outside your home. In case of fire, go to the meeting place. Someone should be sent to phone the fire department.
6. Meet the firefighters when they arrive.
7. Make certain that everyone in your home knows **not to re-enter a burning building.** Firefighters are properly equipped and trained to perform rescue operations.

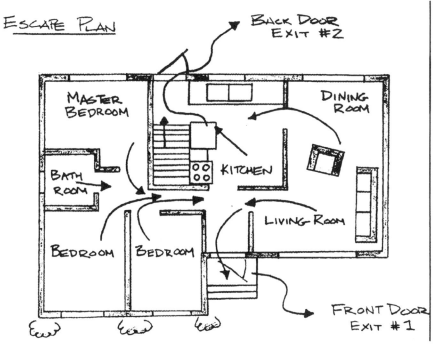

Crawl Low Under Smoke To Your Exit.

If you have to escape a fire through smoke, crawl low, keeping your head 12 to 24 inches (30 to 60 centimeters) above the floor, where the air is cleaner.

Fireplaces

Have your chimney inspected by a professional at least once a year and have it cleaned if necessary. Always use a fire screen, and burn only material appropriate for fireplaces. Never burn trash or paper in a fireplace; burning paper can float up your chimney and onto your roof or into your yard.

Remove ashes in a metal container. Never store ashes in your home. Add wood to fireplaces carefully; sparks can fly into the room while the screen is open.

Candles

Before you light them, put candles in non-tip candle holders. Never burn candles near a Christmas tree or combustible decorations or displays. Keep candles well away from curtains and other combustibles, and never put candles in windows or near exits. Don't leave candles burning unattended or within the reach of small children. Extinguish candles before you leave a room or go to bed.

Christmas Trees

Choose a fresh-cut Christmas tree. If you're not cutting it yourself, buy a tree that's not shedding its needles. Cut the trunk at an angle and install the tree in a large, deep, non-tip stand well away from fireplaces, exits, and heat sources. Be sure to water your tree frequently - check the level daily. Remove your tree promptly if it becomes dry. Store it well away from your home until you can dispose of it. If you use an artificial tree, be sure it's flame-retardant.

WHAT IS CARBON MONOXIDE?

1. Carbon Monoxide (CO) is a colorless, odorless, tasteless, and deadly gas.
2. Called the "silent killer" because it sneaks up on its victims and can take lives without warning.

WHAT CAN YOU DO TO PREVENT A CO HAZARD? YOUR BEST DEFENCE AGAINST CARBON MONOXIDE POISONING IS PREVENTION.

1. Have a qualified service technician check your furnace and other fuel burning equipment at least once a year.
2. Have your chimneys cleaned and inspected at least once a year.
3. Don't idle your vehicle in an attached garage, even with the door open.
4. Make sure all fuel-burning appliances are properly ventilated.
5. Avoid using barbecues or charcoal grills inside the home, tent or camper, or in an unventilated garage.
6. Install a CO detector to the latest standards (UL 2034, CSA 6.19, or IAS 6-96).
7. Follow the manufacturer's instructions as to where to mount a CO detector in your home and test it regularly.

BE AWARE OF THE CO RISKS IN YOUR HOME. YOU CAN INSTALL A DETECTOR AND TAKE PRECAUTIONS TO LESSEN THE POSSIBILITIES OF CO BUILD-UP IN YOUR HOME.

WHAT DO YOU DO IF YOUR CO DETECTOR GOES OFF?

1. Leave the home immediately and call 911 or your local fire department.
2. Remember, an alarm indicates elevated levels of CO in your home. Some people can be exposed to dangerous levels of CO and not feel any symptoms. Regardless of whether you feel symptoms, never ignore the alarm.
FOR MORE INFORMATION ABOUT CARBON MONOXIDE CALL YOUR LOCAL FIRE DEPT.

WHEN IS ICE SAFE?

There is no such thing.

Playing on or around ice-covered bodies of water can be very dangerous. Use extreme caution.

When skating or playing on ice, children should always be supervised by an adult.

Storm retention ponds are not safe recreation areas.

Know the location of the nearest phone in case you need to call for help.

Know the location of a life buoy.

ARE YOU ON THIN ICE?
WHAT DO YOU DO IF YOU FALL IN?

Remain calm.

Call for help.

Do not thrash about.

If you can pull yourself up on the ice crawl a number of feet away from the hole.

Do not stand until you are on firm ground.

Seek shelter, warmth and medical attention if required.

So You Want To Be a Firefighter

FIREMAN GEORGE

Strolling home from school with his mother one warm, spring afternoon, eight-year-old George stopped in his tracks when they came upon a neighborhood house that was on fire.

The bright red fire engines and ambulance had already arrived and there was a flurry of action around the site. Three firefighters were busy taking the long, heavy hose off of the truck and dragging it toward the flaming house, while two other rescuers carefully removed a long ladder and placed it against the second story window. They quickly scurried up the ladder in their long coats, big boots and carrying an axe and chainsaw. Once the men had reached the roof, they began to chop a hole in the roof to allow the smoke to escape.

George and his mother were kept at a safe distance away on the ground with the advice of the police officers on the scene. George squeezed his mother's hand tightly, and thinking he was frightened, she turned to leave and continue on their way home. George quickly stopped her. "Mom, we can't go now! Let's watch and see the firemen put the fire out, please." Her young son pleaded. Looking down, his mother noticed how captivated he was with all the commotion around them. His little head darted from side to side, making sure he wouldn't miss any of the action.

After all the excitement had settled down and the fireman were now cleaning up the site, George was satisfied it was over and he and his mother went home. That night at supper, George could not stop telling his father every detail the firemen had done that day. "That's what I'm going to be one day Dad, a fireman!" George proudly announced.

His father laughed at the enthusiasm in his young boy. "Well then you had better finish your broccoli because firemen must be very strong and healthy." George looked at his plate and grimaced but he slowly opened his mouth and finished his dinner.

That was the beginning of George's life long dream and through his childhood he would only play or read anything that was related to firemen or fire engines. Each year George would beg his Mom to take him to the local fire station for their annual open house where they would welcome the public to come and meet them, sit in the trucks and engines and learn more about fire prevention.

Year after year George would attend until he eventually began telling the firemen about the engines and equipment even before they would have a chance to tell him. He was a welcomed visitor.

Time passed and George never lost his focus on becoming a firefighter. He had grown into a strong, handsome young man and right after graduating high school he applied for Fire College. The closest college was located in Brandon.

Once he was selected, George gave his parents a big hug and boarded the first bus for Brandon. He was full of excitement and anxiety. He had waited so long for this moment and he could hardly believe the time had finally arrived. He knew it would be difficult but he was ready for the challenges that lay ahead.

George had thought he had prepared himself for the grueling and intense course that firefighters had to complete, but night after night as he fell exhausted into bed, he was amazed by the strength and perseverance it took to keep pushing himself.

Brandon Fire College offers training in just about everything a fireman will encounter on a call. First the students must complete a physical test. Some of the physically demanding drills are climbing steep stairs with full gear on which includes 12 1/2 pounds of weight and carrying equipment such as chainsaws without touching the rails.

An endurance test involves dragging a 2 1/2 inch, 100 pound hose up the stairs and into a high rise building. The test goes on and on with drills on forcible entry (chopping down doors or smashing out windows), ladder raise and extension and search for missing bodies (mannequins) in a dark, smoke-filled maze.

George managed to complete all the tasks pretty well but he found the most difficult one was called the Breach and Pull. This drill involves a fireman repeatedly pushing and pulling a long pipe with a hook at the end over his head and into a ceiling. This proved arm strength and even though George was very strong, he felt quite weak at the end of this event.

He also had to learn to overcome his small fear of heights and dark places.

One of the training houses George had to enter was so smoky that he couldn't even see his own feet. He knew he had to stay below the level of heat and smoke, so he crawled on his hands and knees, thankful for his thick gloves, pants and boots. Breathing through his air tube, George had to depend on his other senses besides his eyes. He relied on his ears and listened very carefully for sounds to lead him through the darkness. He successfully completed the task of recovering a body (mannequin) and was proud he had overcome his fears.

George had certainly learned a lot with this course, even some things he didn't even think of before, like learning how buildings are made and how fire will move through walls and rooms of a structure. Even though he had helped his father out in their garage from time to time at home, George had never used a power saw for cutting through metal or wood like he did at Fire College. One of the most interesting and rewarding classes he took was in emergency first aid and how to rescue people. He was so excited every time he successfully brought out a mannequin from one of the burning buildings on the school grounds.

KIDS, DON'T PLAY WITH FIRE!

George didn't realize that each position in the fire department has a nick-name. The Chauffeur is the driver that is responsible for the truck but he can also operate the tall ladder from a pedestal on the truck while two fire fighters ride inside the bucket that is raised up to a very tall building. The Roof Man uses a saw to cut holes in a roof that allows the smoke and flames to get out. The Vent Man is on the ground searching for people in a building by opening doors and breaking windows.

The Nozzle Man must be very strong because he controls the nozzle of the heavy line of the hose while two other firemen hold the hose and spray the water. Even taking the hose off the fire truck is hard work because the hose can be fifty feet long and very heavy, especially when the water begins to shoot through it. The Nozzle Man needs a rest after a few minutes because of the pressure and changes places with the next fireman in line on the hose.

The Fire Chief has a very important job and he always arrives at the scene in a different vehicle from the fire truck. He is easy to spot because he wears a white hat. Using a walkie-talkie radio, he instructs both rigs where to go and what needs to be done, such as where the water hose should go. He also decides if more fire trucks need to be called in to help out with the fire. Several rigs can hook their lines (or hoses) to the first pumper truck to shoot water inside and outside of the building. When the fire is put out and it's time to clean up, the hose is disconnected from the fire hydrant and lifted over the firemen's shoulders to make sure all the water has drained out before they pack it back on the truck.

Once all the physical testing was completed, George settled himself into a desk and prepared for the academic part. This is where he was glad he had paid close attention to his studies in high school because the test involved vocabulary, spelling, numbers, science and basic grade twelve.

Finally the much anticipated day had arrived and George proudly displayed his Level Two certificate in Fire Protection to his parents. Now the next step was to begin his first day at a real fire station.

George's first day at work began with him trying to catch some sleep on a bunk in the firehouse. Firemen sleep in their clothes because when the alarm comes in for a fire, every second counts and getting dressed would take up too much time.

Breaking George's sound sleep was the high pitched sound of the fire bell in the station. A loud speaker announces the emergency's call address and code. A code tells the firemen what kind of fire they can expect. This particular code was called a 10-34, which means a house fire.

George quickly slides down the brass pole because he knows the stairs are too slow and can be dangerous when in a hurry. Jumping into his 'turnout' pants that are sitting on top of his boots also saves time. He slips his feet into his steel plated boots that will protect him from sharp objects, such as nails and broken glass. Next he pulls on his 'turnout' coat that is very heavy because it has three layers of material.

The outer layer will protect him from up to 1,200 degrees Fahrenheit of heat, the next layer is a moisture layer that will keep him dry from water and the third layer is thermal and that will keep his body cool during the intense heat of a fire. And of course his jacket has lots of pockets to carry all the equipment he might need. Yellow stripes on the outside of the jacket glow in the dark, so he can be easily spotted. Thick leather gloves protect his hands and a thin hood and strong helmet will make sure his head doesn't get injured from falling debris. Next George adjusts his face mask and 25 pound air tank on his back and hops into the waiting fire engine. He has a lot of clothes to put on but because he has had so much practice, George can do it in just a couple of minutes.

George was a firefighter for over twenty years before he retired. He saved many lives and unfortunately some he could not. Now George goes to schools and tells children about fire prevention, like not playing with matches and making sure their homes have smoke alarms. Sometimes when he looks out into a classroom of children, George can see a child with the same enthusiasm he once had and knows that someday this person will also be a firefighter, just like he was.

THE END

The following pages are true stories of Firefighter Heroism

DOWN UNDER

Mark and Matthew had been warned many times by their parents not to play in or around the new housing development. Even the construction company building the homes had put up a fence with warning signs that it was dangerous and to keep out.

Mark and Matthew would ride their bikes past the site each day on their way home from school and every time they would stop, get off of their bikes, press their faces against the chain-linked fence and try to figure out a way to enter the site without getting caught.

"It looks so cool in there; there must be some way we can sneak in without anyone catching us," said Mark to his friend. "I know what you mean. This place would be so great to play hide and seek. I bet there's probably a dinosaur bone or maybe some kind of buried treasure in some of those deep holes," replied Matthew as he turned his head from side to side searching for a way in.

41

Later on that evening Mark watched his dad work on his latest hobby project in the garage. When his father took out some wire cutters to cut through some thick cable, Mark's eyes widened and knew how he and his friend could get through the chain-linked fence at the construction site.

The next morning, both boys told their mothers they had to stay after school to finish a science project they had been working on. But they didn't stay after school; they instead went straight to the new housing development. They hid their bikes in a nearby bush and Mark unzipped his backpack to reveal the wire cutters he had taken from his dad's garage.

Both boys had to use their hands and press tightly on the cutters but they finally managed to cut through enough small triangles in the fence to squeeze their small eleven-year-old bodies through.

Once inside, they scurried around the lot, hopping over piles of dirt and looking under large boulders, hopping to find a missing bone or gold coins. While Mark had bent down examining a small stone he had found, he faintly heard his name being called by Matthew.

Curious, he stood up and slowly walked around the site calling out his friend's name, trying to follow his voice to his location. His heart began to pound when he came upon a wooden plank that had a hole broken into it. Moving the plank aside to reveal a large, deep cavity in the earth, Mark bent down on his knees and carefully leaned over the darkened site and called Matthew's name out.

"I'm down here!" yelled Matthew. "I fell through a piece of wood and I think my wrist is broken, it hurts really bad," he whimpered. "Mark hurry and get me out of here, it's really scary and dark down here." His friend pleaded.

Mark jumped up. "I'll call 911 Matthew, Hang in there! We'll get you out. I'll be right back!" he shouted as he raced through the hole in the fence, hopped on his bike and rode home faster than he had ever gone before.

Within five minutes, sirens were heard screaming and there was a flurry of action at the construction site. Four fire trucks, an ambulance, both boys' parents and the construction engineer were all gathered around the gapping hole. Surveying the situation, the Fire Captain decided to call on the Trench Rescue Team. These firemen were specially trained in retrieving people from situations just like this.

The engineer advised them the hole was approximately fifteen feet deep. Leaning over the edge, a fireman called down to Matthew. It was so dark down there that no one could see the boy until he looked straight up at them. Matthew's entire body was covered in dirt and the only thing the rescuers could see were two little round eyes peering out of the darkness.

Nightfall would soon be arriving, so the rescue team knew they had to act promptly to take advantage of the remaining daylight. Digging another hole beside Matthew's would seem to be the easiest option but the Trench Rescuers feared that because the hole was located on a slope, the action of the digging might cause the earth to collapse and bury the boy.

They quickly threw down a rope and instructed Matthew to secure it tightly under each arm. It had been over an hour since Matthew had fallen down the hole. Covered in dirt, thirsty and tired, the young boy slowly tried to tuck the rope under each arm. When the team began to pull the rope up, after only a few feet Matthew lost his strength and his arm slipped from the rope hold.

Falling back down into the darkened hole, Matthew began to cry in fear of never getting out. The rescue team then decided that although he would be a very tight squeeze, one of them would have to carefully repel down and try to reach him.

What seemed like hours were actually only moments in time as the fireman dropped himself into the hole, being careful not to disturb the earth on the sides and causing more dirt to fall on the young boy. He eventually made his way down and was right above Matthew. The fireman managed to securely fasten the rope around Matthew and he signed for the other firemen to begin to pull them up to safety.

Matthew was so relieved when he finally saw daylight. The ambulance attendants instantly took over and began cleaning the boy off and checking his vital signs. Matthew's parents were so happy to see their son, as was Mark.

Matthew was released from the hospital the next day sporting a new cast on his broken wrist. Both Mark and Matthew knew they were not out of the woods yet. Two police officers stopped by their homes and explained how they could be arrested for trespassing. The officers also informed the boys how they not only put themselves in danger, but also the many people rescuing them. It was a dangerous situation for everyone.

The boys definitely learned their lesson, but they felt they needed to warn others about how serious trespassing on construction sites can be, so they asked their school if they could talk to the students in the gym one day. Their message was well received by all the classmates and the boys were even asked to go to other schools to share their frightening story, and hopefully prevent this from happening again.

The End

44

Boy's Best Friend

Jake and his dog Sam were inseparable. They lived in a small town where no one was a stranger, and each day when the two best friends strolled down the street, everyone would smile and say hello. Sometimes they would even stop to give Sam a special dog treat.

So when the 911 call came in to Fire Station 11 about a young boy and his dog stranded on an ice flow in the lake, the firemen knew immediately who they were.

The Surface Rescue Squad, which was made up of specialty trained firefighters rushed to the scene where they came upon two shivering souls, wet and sitting on a small piece of ice surrounded by frigid water.

They quickly took the Zodiak Rescue Boat off of the fire truck and inflated it in seconds. Four men pulled on emersion suits that would keep them dry and warm if they had to enter the cold water. Slowly guiding the Zodiak through large pieces of broken ice on the lake, the firemen tried to get the boat close enough for Jake and Sam to crawl into but unfortunately the ice floe they were on had sharp edges that prevented the boat from getting close enough.

Jake's lips were blue, and both he and his dog couldn't stop shivering. One of the rescuers tied a rope around his waist before slipping into the water. If a piece of ice floated between him and the boat, the situation could become dangerous, but with the rope tethered to his waist, his partner could pull him back to safety.

Once the fireman swam up to the ice floe, he instructed Jake to carefully crawl to him so he could carry him back to the boat. Jake didn't want to leave his dog but was assured by the rescuer that he would come back for Sam, and he did just that.

Once the two were safely on shore and wrapped in blankets, Jake explained how he thought the ice was thick enough to walk on, but before he knew it, a big piece had broken away and they both fell in. It was hard but Jake managed to crawl onto a piece of the ice floe and pull his dog Sam up onto it with him.

After carefully listening to the dangers about getting too close to frozen water, Jake knew he would never try such a stunt again and would make sure he told all his friends about his experience so they wouldn't have to go through such a frightening experience like he and Sam did.

KEEP GAS AWAY FROM THE FURNACE!

The End

Hazmat

HAZMAT is short for the Hazards Material Squad that some fire fighters are specially trained in dealing with dangerous chemicals. This was the team that was sent to Shawn's house when his mother phoned in the 911 call.

The situation began with Shawn and his little brother Bobby deciding to play scientists in the laundry room. Six-year-old Shawn and four-year-old Bobby had watched their favorite show on television earlier that day and were fascinated by a science experiment. They watched a man dressed in a white lab coat mix two liquids together in glass beakers. Smoke instantly began billowing over the top of one of the glass containers. It looked really cool to the boys and they decided to do the same experiment at home, unaware that the television show only used water and dry ice to make the smoke.

Opening a cupboard beside the washing machine, Shawn found two white plastic bottles. Both boys knelt on the floor and watched as Shawn poured one of the bottles into the other one. Within a few short moments, the boys jumped back when they heard a loud POP from inside one of the containers.

As soon as the chemicals were mixed together they ignited and instantly melted the plastic bottle. Upstairs in the kitchen, their mother also heard the noise and quickly ran downstairs into the laundry room. As she entered the room, her two frightened sons quickly ran past her, rubbing their eyes and flying up the stairs and out the back door for fresh air.

Entering the laundry room, the boys' mother instantly noticed the strong smell of toxic vapors creating a burning sensation in her nose. She immediately called 911 and told them the situation. Once the HAZMAT team arrived, two men began opening all the windows in the house while one firefighter tried to determine what chemicals were mixed by reading the containers' labels and using a small chemical testing machine. Hooking up a small hose, the laundry room was quickly soaked to prevent further fires and reduce the strong vapors in the air.

Once the situation was under control, the firemen went outside and spoke with Shawn and Bobby about how dangerous mixing liquids together can be. Both boys knew they were lucky this time and had learned their lesson, and so did their mother. The next day, she put away all the hazardous and dangerous liquids in her house, so the boys wouldn't be tempted to do this again.

The End

Fallen Friend

Nick & Michael loved to go to the river's edge and skip rocks, seeing whose rock would make the most bounces on top of the water. After awhile, this became boring to the two nine-year-olds, so they decided to try and skip the rocks from on top of the bridge.

Michael leaned forward, resting his chest on the cement ledge of the bridge, twisted his wrist to the right, and threw his flat smooth rock into the water, causing it to skip three times. "I've got the record so far! Did you see it skip three whole times Nick?"

"Yes, I saw it but wait until you see how many times my rock skips!" said Nick as he began to crawl up onto the bridge's ledge. "What are you doing Nick? That's too dangerous! Get down from there!" demanded a frightened Michael.

"Don't worry, I'll be careful," Nick replied as he cautiously placed his footing and stood up tall. Nick looked down and felt a little dizzy when he realized how high he was but he was determined to skip his rock the furthest. He took his smooth, triangle shaped stone and pitched it into the river but before he knew it, he had lost his balance and fell off the bridge, landing onto the embankment below.

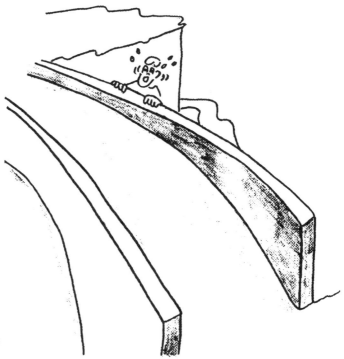

"Nick! Are you okay?" screamed his friend as he watched in horror from the bridge above. Nick lay very still below with blood trickling down the side of his head.

Michael knew he had to get help right away, so he ran as fast as his feet could carry him to the nearest adult and asked him to call 911.

In less than four minutes, two

fire trucks and an ambulance raced to the scene. The Technical Rescue squad quickly assessed the situation and took control.

As an ambulance attendant tried to comfort Michael, the firemen quickly tied one end of the two ropes around the closest tree trunk and threw the other ends over the bridge, dropping them beside an unconscious Nick. One rope was called a static rope that doesn't have any stretch to it and that was the one the fireman repelled down on. The other rope is called the safety rope that is there in case the fireman needs help. Each rope can hold up to 9,000 lbs. and is replaced by a new one at the fire station after each use to make sure they are safe and lift just about any amount of weight.

"Nick, can you hear me?" said the fireman as he leaned over the youngster's body. Nick's feet slowly began to move and soon his eyes opened. Looking up into the stranger's face, Nick seemed confused. "What happened? Where am I?" he asked in a weak voice. "You fell off the bridge and we're going to get you out of here, but first I want to see if you're hurt any where else." After the fireman did a quick evaluation and was satisfied Nick didn't break or seriously injure himself, he looked up at the other firemen and told them to send the harness down.

Resembling a big diaper, the fireman gently placed Nick's arms and legs securely in the harness and gave the nod for the other firemen to pull him up.

Nick was taken to the hospital to make sure he didn't have any other injuries other than the small cut on his forehead. "You were very lucky son," said the doctor. "I hope you have learned your lesson from this."
Nick smiled at his parents and his friend Michael as they stood by his bedside. "I promise never to do anything that foolish again. I guess you win the rock skipping contest Michael," an exhausted Nick whispered. "Who cares about that silly contest, as long as you're okay is all that matters." Everyone in the room agreed.

Fire Fighters often save the lives of strangers but sometimes they are called upon to save one of their own.

Ted Kuryluk and Lloyd Stankey performed CPR on a colleague who had a heart attack yesterday while giving a tour of the Fire Service Museum of Winnipeg and saved his life.

"I gave him mouth-to-mouth, and Ted started compression. We're a pretty good team, I guess," said Stanley, a retired captain.

Retired firefighter Bill Mitchell, 72, was leading a group of Grade 5 and 6 students on a tour of the historic fire hall at 56 Maple St. about 9:45 a.m. when he dropped to the ground after walking up a flight of stairs.

"During the collapse, as I attended to him he was just gasping for air, then it ceased," said Lieut. Ted Kuryluk who called 911 as soon as he saw Mitchell.

"There weren't any vital signs at all."

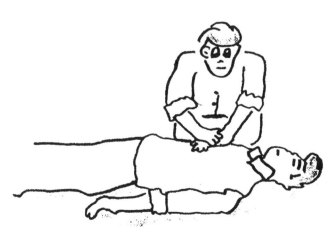

The two men performed CPR and continued until emergency services arrived and were able to restore Mitchell's breathing.

"The jury's still out on how he's going to be. The last word is that he was breathing on his own, but he's still in intensive care," Kuryluk said.

Both men are trained first responders and have done similar

deeds many times on the job. Kuryluk, 49, has been a firefighter for 26 years and works out of the No. 11 Fire Station on Portage Avenue and Berry Street.

Stankey, 71, retired in 1989 after 32 years on the job and has known Mitchell for over 30 years.

The modest pair don't think they did anything special.

"You do what you have to do," Stankey said. "It's automatic, I guess you could say."

"We usually do it for other people, we don't usually do it for our own," Kuryluk added.

Mitchell, a member of the fire department for 31 years before retiring in 1987, remained in hospital last night.

He has volunteered at the Point Douglas Museum since it opened last year in the city's longest standing fire station, which opened in 1903 and was the oldest operating fire station in Canada before closing in 1990.

HOSPITALS CAN HELP YOU, IF YOU'RE HURT

When new life enters the world sometimes there is a firefighter on the scene

FOUR firefighters came to the rescue of a baby girl who just couldn't wait to be born.

Deb, was enroute to Health Sciences Centre around 9:30 a.m. when she realized she just wasn't going to make it. The friends driving her to the hospital pulled their van over on Main Street near Burrows Avenue and called an ambulance.

Al Procter and his first responder unit — including Curtis McClintock, Darcy Funk and Dale Dreilich —were first on the scene.

"We got there, there were a couple of other folks with her, waving their arms, in advanced stages of panic and they told us she was delivering," Procter said. "We always hear they're delivering. But she was delivering,

"The baby's head was crowning, and we delivered the baby."

Deb said her daughter, whom she hasn't named yet, was about two weeks early and weighed eight pounds. She arrived while her mother lay in the back of the mini-van.

"It was very, very cold," Procter said. "We wrapped her in lots of blankets."

The paramedics arrived shortly after the baby was born and took mother and daughter, Deb's fourth child, to St. Boniface General Hospital where they were resting last night.

"It was kind of a treat for us." said Procter, who works out of Station 6 at McGregor and Redwood. "We see a lot of trauma, bad situations. It was nice to get a call, one where it's upbeat."

Firefighters rescue dogs too

WINNIPEG firefighters ventured onto the ice of the Assiniboine River yesterday for a rescue that was doggone dramatic.

Charlie, a 14-year-old golden retriever, had fallen into the freezing water early yesterday near Ridgedale Crescent in the Charleswood area. The dog's howls were so loud, firefighters could hear them 200 yards away. "His eyes had a look that kind of said, 'Get me out of here, please," said Lionel Charron, one of 12 firefighters who responded to the call.

The dog was fighting for his life when Winnipeg firefighters found him, his head barely above the water, while his paws desperately scratched the icy river banks.

Firefighters said the dog's long toe nails helped him grab on to the ice. Earlier in the morning, owner Bob Hannah had let him out before going to work but had forgotten to let him back in.

Lieut. Chuck Jonasson of the Winnipeg Fire Paramedic Service estimated the dog had been in the water for about 30 minutes when his crew found him.

Dressed in water suits and hooked to a safety rope, firefighters Joe Lepiesco and Lionel ventured onto the ice to attempt a rescue. Crawling on his belly, Lionel grabbed the dog's collar and pulled it out of the water.

"He was soaking wet and shivering, and he couldn't walk, but he was happy to be out," said Lionel.

The firefighters took Charlie to the Charleswood Veterinarian Clinic, where he was treated for hypothermia. "It's quite remarkable, he's a very lucky dog," said veterinarian Lisa Sawka. "His coat is very thin and he's arthritic and so old for a golden retriever."

In human years, Charlie is about 90 years old, Lisa said, adding credit should go to the firefighters who saved his life. "It was quite a scene — these men walking in, shivering themselves, with a dog wrapped up in a blanket in their arms," she said.

Yesterday, Capt. Bob Richen cautioned Winnipeggers to stay away from the city's rivers, creeks and retention ponds — it's just too early to venture onto icy surfaces. "We had six or eight calls today of children going too close to the ponds," he said. "The ice is just starting to freeze so it's best to stay away until it's posted as safe."

Wagging his tail, Charlie was reunited with best pal, 11-year-old Bobby Hannah, after a five-hour stay at the clinic.

"We were very worried, we love him very much," said Hannah from his home last night. "He's sleeping a lot now, but he's old and he likes to sleep."

The End

Priceless Value of a Pet

The fire fighter could see the column of smoke when they left the station. A mobile home was on fire and it was getting bigger fast! As the screaming truck went through town and up to the house, the fire fighter had only one thing on his mind - please don't let anyone get hurt.

Pulling up in front, the fire fighter could see the house was completely on fire. Nothing could make it out of that inferno. Sitting in front of the house was a car with a sad lady in it. She was the owner and she was seeing everything she had go up in flames and smoke. The fire fighter knew all that could be done was to put out the fire and go through the ashes to see if anything was left.

It took a good hour to bring the fire under control so the fire fighter could help go through what was left. Stepping on the burned boards of the front porch, a sound was heard that didn't belong. Looking under the porch, the fire fighter saw two small eyes looking back. A kitten!!! Wet, and a bit singed, the little fellow was wailing at the top of his lungs. The fire fighter carefully reached under the porch and brought him out. Knowing the little fellow had been through more than one of his nine lives, the fire fighter went to find the lady who owned the house.

Upon seeing the kitten, the lady burst into tears, knowing she did have something left of her life after all. All her worldly goods were gone, but a little kitten still depended on her for his next steps in life. All was not lost as a bond was formed between the kitten and the lady. The fire fighter, knowing a good thing had happened in the middle of a terrible tragedy, slept well that night. His job had been done as best as it could be and his maker rewarded him with thanks from a grateful lady and a loud meow from one of God's creatures saved.

Charles Bratcher
1ST Asst. Chief
Groesbeck Fire Dept.,Texas